The
Science of a
Spring

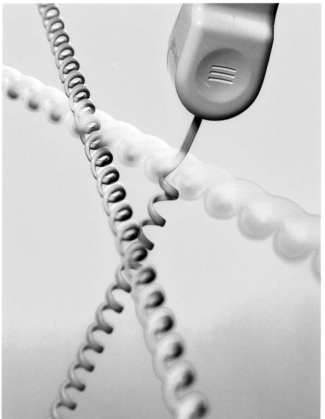

John Stringer

RAINTREE
STECK-VAUGHN
PUBLISHERS
A Steck-Vaughn Company

Austin, Texas

www.steck-vaughn.com

Science World

Other titles in the series:

The Science of
Gravity

The Science of a
Light Bulb

The Science of
Noise

Picture acknowledgments
The publishers would like to thank the following for allowing their pictures to be reproduced in this book:
Action-Plus/Steve Bardens 7; Bubbles/Pauline Cutler *cover* [inset middle], 6; Martyn F. Chillmaid 4 (bottom);
Eye Ubiquitous/NASA 19 (bottom), /Paul Seheult 25 (bottom); Getty Images/Dan Bosler 26, /Chuck Davis 21,
/Mark Harwood *title page*, /Renee Lynn *cover* [main], 27, /World Perspectives 14; Robert Harding 24 (bottom),
/Eric Sanford 9; Paul Humphrey/Discovery Books 15 (bottom)Impact/Garaini Lewis 10; Popperphoto 22, /Bob
Thomas 8 (top); Science Photo Library 19 (top), /Jerrican Aurel 24 (top), /Sheila Terry 28; /Jerome Yeats 8
(middle); Trip/H. Rogers *contents page*; John Walmsley 18; Wayland Picture Library *cover* [inset top], 4 (top and
middle), 8 (bottom) 12, 15 (top), 17, 25 (top and middle). **Illustrator:** Peter Bull

Published by Raintree Steck-Vaughn Publishers,
an imprint of Steck-Vaughn Company

Printed in Italy. Bound in the United States.
1 2 3 4 5 6 7 8 9 0 04 03 02 01 00

Library of Congress Cataloging-in-Publication
Data
Stringer, John.
The science of a spring / John Stringer.
      p.   cm.—(Science world)
      Includes bibliographical references and index.
      Summary: Explains why springs act the way
      they do, based on elementary concepts of
      physics.
      ISBN 0-7398-1322-6
      1. Springs (Mechanism)—Juvenile literature.
      2. Force and energy—Juvenile literature.
      [1. Springs (Mechanism). 2. Force and energy.]
      I. Title. II. Series.
TJ210.S74   2000
621.8'24—dc21   99-36210

Contents

Types of Springs

Think about springs. What do you know about them? Springs are found in many unexpected places.

There are probably springs in your bed and in your clock. ▼

▲ Springs are in a stapler. Paper clips are also types of springs.

A spring is even on the ▶ shutter of each floppy disk!

In fact, you are probably surrounded by springs.

How does a stapler work?

If you look inside a stapler, you will see two types of springs. A flat leaf spring lifts the arm back after you have stapled something. And a long coil spring pushes the next staple into place.

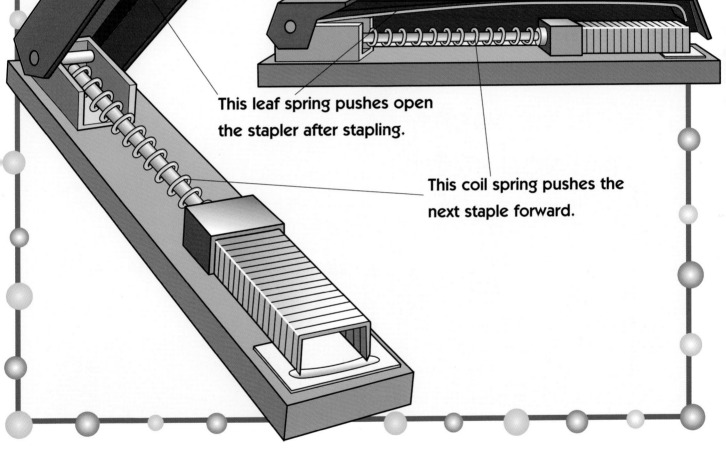

This leaf spring pushes open the stapler after stapling.

This coil spring pushes the next staple forward.

Shapes of springs

There are two main types of springs: leaf springs and coil springs. Leaf springs are flat pieces of metal, and coil springs are coiled pieces of metal.

Springs that squash and bend

When you push some springs, you squeeze them or bend them, and they change shape. Springs that are squashed or bent always try to go back to their original shape.

What happens when you stand on a pogo stick?

A pogo stick has a coiled spring at the bottom. When you jump on a pogo stick, the spring is squashed by your weight. When it's squashed, the spring jumps back into its original shape and bounces you into the air.

Springs that bend are called leaf springs. Leaf springs bend and then return to how they were. You can see them clearly on car trailers and on some house trailers.

The leaf spring on this trailer ▶ is pressed down when the trailer is loaded.

leaf spring

Beds and chairs use springs that press down so that you can get comfortable. Cars and other vehicles and some mountain bikes use coiled springs near the wheels. These make you more comfortable when traveling over bumpy surfaces.

This mountain bike ▶ has springs attached to its frame near the wheels. These soften the bumps for the rider and make the journey more enjoyable.

Springs that stretch

Some springs can be stretched. Like springs that squash, springs that are stretched try to get back to their original shape.

There are many stretchy springs around you. They are in baby bouncers and the straps that hold objects onto your bike. They are used in gymnasium equipment, such as rowing machines. They are even in your clothes. Without the stretchy material in the waistband, your pants would fall down!

▲ This baby bouncer has a springy metal frame. It bends, gently bouncing the baby.

This rowing machine has long coil springs ▶ on the foot blocks. When you push, you stretch them. When you relax, the springs pull the blocks back.

The stretchy clothes on this gymnast move ▼ with her body. She even has a stretchy hair band to hold back her hair.

If you were to leap from a crane with a bungee rope tied to your ankles, the rope would stretch. As it stretches, the rope slows you down. And it keeps you from hitting the ground. The bungee rope is stretched most as you reach the end of your fall. Then it begins pulling you back.

How long does a bungee rope stretch?

The world's record bungee jump was from a helicopter.
The bungee rope stretched from 820 ft. (250 m) to more than 1,965 ft. (600 m).

Forces and Springs

Springs work because of forces. To understand how springs work, we need to learn about these forces. A force is a push or a pull. The best way to show how forces work is to use pictures. We can show the directions of the forces at work, using arrows. We can also show the size of the force—the longer the arrow, the stronger the force.

When forces are balanced

When there is no movement, forces are still at work, but they are balanced.

▼ These two sumo wrestlers aren't moving, but you can tell there are forces at work. The men are sweating and straining. We know that they are both using the same amount of force because they are not moving. If one of the sumo wrestlers stopped pushing so hard, the forces would be out of balance. And the other wrestler would push him backward.

These two tug-of-war teams aren't moving, so the forces must be balanced. Both teams are using the same amount of pulling force. If more people joined the team on the right, the forces would be unbalanced. Then the right team's pull would be stronger.

Once the forces become unbalanced, the team with the stronger pull can win. It pulls the team with the weaker pull over a line between them.

It's not so easy to show the ▶ forces acting on this ball. There are two forces at work: a pulling force, called gravity, and a pushing force. Gravity is pulling the ball down toward the center of the earth. So why doesn't the ball go down? Something is stopping it. The ground is pushing back on the ball. Gravity and the push of the ground are in balance. The ball stays where it is!

Gravity

Push back from ground

A book on a table is being ▼ pulled down by gravity. The table is pushing back to keep the book where it is. The arrows show these forces.

Gravity

Push back from table

Are hard objects springy?

When you squeeze a hard object, such as a table leg or a stone, its hard surface pushes back. It changes a little, but it looks as if it stays in much the same shape.

However, even hard surfaces, such as steel and glass, are slightly springy! If something pushes down on a hard surface, it acts a bit like a very stiff trampoline. Objects bounce when they fall and hit something. They also change shape a tiny bit and spring back into shape.

▼ Glass marbles bounce because they change shape a tiny bit as they hit the floor.

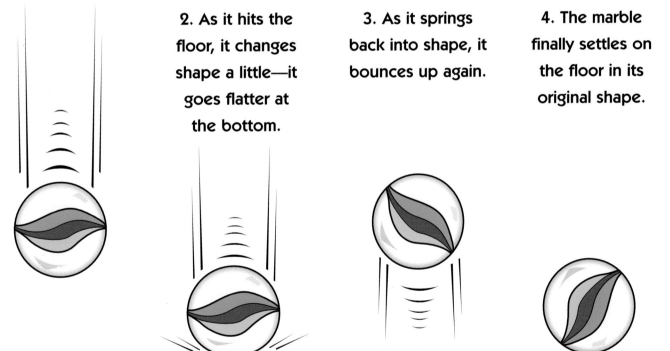

2. As it hits the floor, it changes shape a little—it goes flatter at the bottom.

3. As it springs back into shape, it bounces up again.

4. The marble finally settles on the floor in its original shape.

1. A marble falls to the floor.

The faster an object can spring back into shape, the higher it will bounce. Power balls made of springy plastic get their shape back quickly and bounce very high.

When forces are unbalanced

Sometimes when forces are unbalanced, there is movement. A rocket blasting off from Cape Canaveral is being held back by the downward pull of gravity. But gravity is a weaker force than the mighty upward force of the rocket engines. The forces are unbalanced, so the rocket climbs into the sky.

This rocket will use unbalanced forces to blast out of the earth's atmosphere.▼

Sometimes, when forces are unbalanced, objects change shape.

Try squeezing a block of wood or ▶ metal—these are things that push back hard.

◀ When you squeeze modeling clay, the clay pushes back but not enough to keep it from changing shape. If the clay pushed back as hard as you squeezed, you would hardly change its shape.

When you squeeze or stretch a spring, the forces are unbalanced. The spring changes shape. But when you stop squeezing or stretching, your force stops acting. Then the spring's force jumps it back to shape.

▲ When a spring stays in the same shape, the forces will be balanced. You may feel the spring pushing into you.

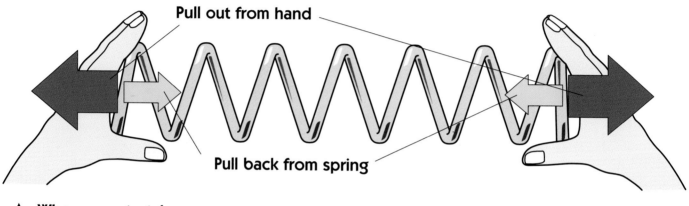

Pull out from hand

Pull back from spring

▲ When you stretch a spring, you are using a stronger pulling force than the pull back from the spring.

Push out from hand

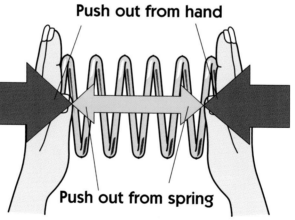

Push out from spring

◄ When you press a spring, you are using a stronger pushing force than the pull back from the spring.

The spring returns to ▶ its original shape if you let it go.

Will a spring stretch forever?

A spring will not stretch forever. A spring reaches the point where it will no longer stretch. Scientists call this point the elastic limit.

What happens when you stretch a spring over its elastic limit?

You can see what happens when you bend modeling clay too far. The boy is bending the clay to a point where bending it any farther will cause it to break. You can see the cracks.

When a spring reaches its elastic limit, any more force will change it for good. It will not go back to its original shape. If you go on stretching a spring, it snaps.

Weight and the earth's pull

The earth pulls on every object. The amount of this pull is called the object's weight.

How do we measure a pull force?

A newton meter measures the size of a pull force. It has a spring inside so that it can measure the pull on an object. The earth pulls down on the object, and the object pulls on the spring. The stretched spring moves a pointer that shows how much the object weighs.

A newton meter can also measure how much pull force is needed to pull an object along a surface. When you pull an object along with a newton meter, you are measuring the force needed to move it. Forces are measured in newtons.

Sir Isaac Newton

Newtons are named after Sir Isaac Newton, an English scientist who lived from 1642 to 1727. One famous story tells of how he watched an apple fall to the ground. This event started him thinking about the force of gravity and why everything falls down to the ground, not sideways or up.

A 1 kg bag of sugar is pulled down toward the earth with a force of 10 newtons. The earth pulls down on a mass of 100g with a force of about 1 newton. One newton is about the weight of a medium-sized apple.

The earth's pull ▶ gives us weight. Without it we would float into space.

Springs All Around Us

We know that springs work because of forces and that they can be bent, squeezed, or stretched. Would you recognize the springs in use around you?

Are you sitting comfortably?

When you sit on a soft chair or lie on a bed, you are squeezing some springs. As you first sit down, the forces are unbalanced. Your weight is greater than the push back from the springs. The springs get shorter until they can't be squeezed anymore. The forces have become balanced because the springs push back on you as hard as you are pushing down on them. You are sitting comfortably. When you stand up, the springs return to their original size.

◀ You can see how the springs are supporting the girl's weight in the chair. They help her sit in comfort.

Some chairs and beds work by stretching springs, rather than by squashing them. There are elastic bands or springs across the frames, which stretch when you sit down.

Can we stop buildings from cracking in earthquakes?

In parts of the world that have earthquakes, tall buildings are built on springs. The springs absorb the force of the earthquake and keep a building from breaking up (as in this picture) and falling down.

What absorbs the bumps?

You may travel in a car, a bus, or a train. If it had no springs, you would be jarred by every bump. Your journey would be uncomfortable, and you would be very sore at the end of it!

▲ This vehicle is designed with springs and shock absorbers that will make even the most bumpy journey comfortable.

The coil springs on a car take up the force of the bumps. The bumps cannot be felt as much in the car. But springs alone would make the car bounce. Cars have shock absorbers that slow down the movement of the springs and keep you from bouncing up and down!

Coil springs on cars are between the axles and the rest of the car. When the car is loaded, the springs are squeezed. They smooth out the bumps. Shock absorbers keep the car from bouncing.

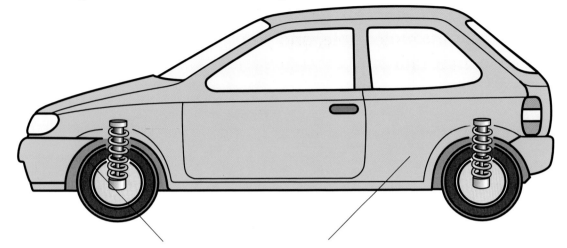

The springs are between the wheel axles and the rest of the car.

The coil spring is slightly squeezed on a flat road.

The coil spring is squeezed as the car bounces over the bumps.

Springing back into shape

There are many objects that use springs that spring back into shape. Springy objects can give us a lot of fun.

▼ When you pull back on a bow, you are using a spring. The pulling force of your arm changes the shape of the bow. The bow slowly bends like a big leaf spring. When you let go, the arrow is fired as the bow springs back into its original shape.

▲ When you jump on a trampoline, it acts like a big spring. It springs back into shape and bounces you into the air.

When you wind a clock or mechanical watch, you are winding a spring. As it gradually unwinds, it will turn the hands of the clock and tell you the time.

◄ This clock has a key at the back. You can turn it to wind the spring inside.

Clockwork toys were ► very popular before electric motors and batteries became cheaper. The springs inside them made parts move.

▼ The inside of a windup clock looks like this. You can see a long metal ribbon coiled tight where a key has turned to wind it. It is made to unwind slowly onto the round metal cylinder. It turns all the gears to make the clock work.

Your springy body

Your body is full of springs and stretchy parts. If it were not, you would have to move around like a robot. You wouldn't be able to jump, and you could not absorb the shock of landing.

▲ When you run, your foot hits the ground with a force. That force is two to three times your body weight. If you ran in a marathon, your foot would hit the ground like this 25,000 times. Your ankles and knees would be hurt without some sort of body springs.

Do animals have springs?

Animals need springy parts inside them, too. Tigers need to be able to run and jump to catch food.

A tiger's legs are the most powerful parts of its body. The tiger relies on a sharp burst of speed and a strong jump to kill its prey. The "springs" in a tiger's legs absorb the force of its jump.

There are bags of fluid in your joints that act like springs, absorbing some of this shock. However, they cannot stand endless pounding. For this reason, you should wear padded springy shoes when playing sports. Sneakers are designed to absorb forces.

Springs in locks

All locks work by using springs, from padlocks to your front-door lock.

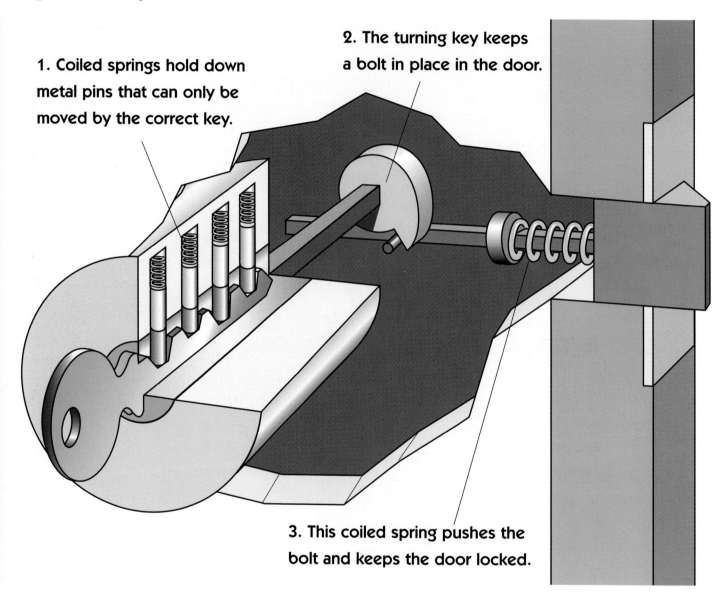

1. Coiled springs hold down metal pins that can only be moved by the correct key.

2. The turning key keeps a bolt in place in the door.

3. This coiled spring pushes the bolt and keeps the door locked.

The lock on your front door contains a lot of tiny springs. They are above a row of metal pins. Only the pattern of your door key will push the springs back and line up the pins. Then the lock will turn.

As the lock turns, it pulls in the bolt locking the door to the wall. The door opens. When you let go of your key, another spring pushes the bolt back.

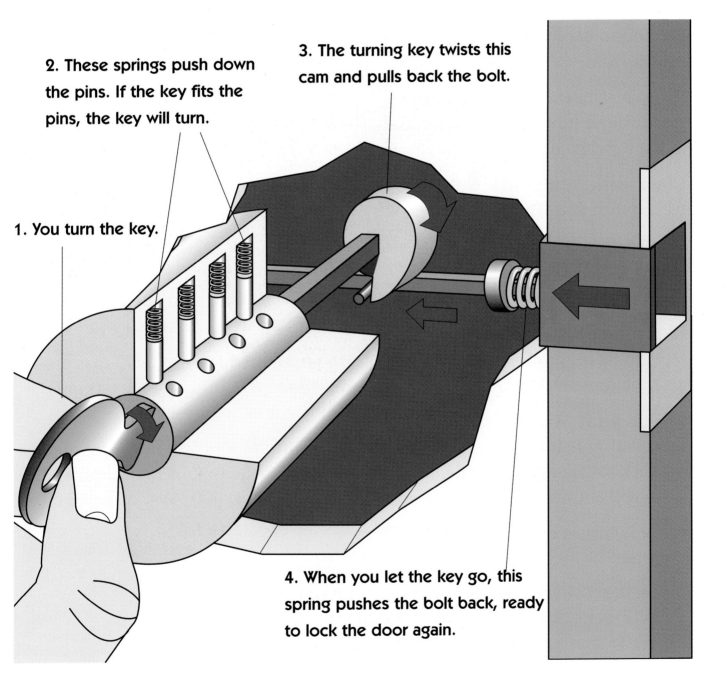

2. These springs push down the pins. If the key fits the pins, the key will turn.

3. The turning key twists this cam and pulls back the bolt.

1. You turn the key.

4. When you let the key go, this spring pushes the bolt back, ready to lock the door again.

Glossary

Axles The poles on which a wheel turns, for example, in a car.

Balanced forces Two forces that are equal and act in opposition to each other.

Cam A wheel that turns around-and-around movement into up-and-down movement.

Clockwork A machine with a coil spring that you wind.

Coil spring A spring that winds around and around and can be pushed and pulled.

Elastic Something that is able to go back to its original shape or length after being stretched or pressed.

Elastic limit A spring at its elastic limit will not stretch any farther and go back to its original shape. More force will change its shape for good.

Forces Pushes or pulls between objects.

Gravity This force is the earth's pull on everything. Every object has a force of gravity, but the earth's is by far the largest.

Leaf springs Flat springs that bend when pushed or pulled.

Mass The amount of matter in an object.

Newton (N) The unit we use to measure force, named after Sir Isaac Newton.

Shock absorbers On a car a tube filled with fluid that keeps the springs from bouncing too much.

Unbalanced forces Two forces that are unequal, and one force is greater than the other.

Weight Weight is a force. An object's weight is the pull of the earth on it. The measure of its weight depends on its mass.

Further Information

Books to read

Glover, David. *Springs* (Simple Machines). Des Plaines, IL: Heinemann Library, 1997.

Grimshaw, Caroline. *Machines*. Chicago: World Book, 1997.

Jennings, Terry. *Forces and Machines* (Making Science Work). Austin, TX: Raintree Steck-Vaughn, 1996.

Oxlade, Chris. *Car* (Take It Apart). Parsippany, NJ: Silver Burdett Press, 1997.

————. *Machines* (Young Scientist Concepts and Projects). Milwaukee, WI: Gareth Stevens, 1998.

Web sites to visit

http://ericir.syr.edu/Projects/Newton/newtonalpha
This site contains many interesting science lessons.

www.lsc.org
This is the home page of the Liberty Science Center.

www.discoveryplace.org
This is the home page of Discovery Place.

Places to visit

Liberty Science Center, Liberty State Park, Phillip Street, Jersey City, NJ (Tel: 201-200-1000). This outstanding science museum has hands-on activities guided by the museum staff.

Discovery Place, 301 North Tryon Street, Charlotte, NC (Tel: 1-800-935-0553). This is an award-winning science and technology museum, featuring hands-on experiments.

Index

Numbers in **bold** refer to pictures as well as text.